WYNDMERE

Wyndmere

POEMS BY CAROL MUSKE

UNIVERSITY OF PITTSBURGH PRESS

Published by the University of Pittsburgh Press, Pittsburgh, Pa. 15260
Copyright © 1985, Carol Muske
All rights reserved
Feffer and Simons, Inc., London
Manufactured in the United States of America

Library of Congress Cataloging in Publication Data

Muske, Carol, 1945-
  Wyndmere.

  (Pitt poetry series)
  I. Title. II. Series.
PS3563.U837W9 1985   811'.54   84-19565
ISBN 0-8229-3503-1
ISBN 0-8229-5365-X (pbk.)

The author and publisher wish to express their grateful acknowledgement to the following publications in which some of these poems, in varying forms, first appeared: *The American Poetry Review* ("Afterwards," "Coming Over Coldwater," "A Former Love, a Lover of Form," "Illness as Metaphor," "Panis Angelicus," "Unheard Of," "White Key," and "Wyndmere, Windemere"); *Columbia Magazine* ("Blood Hour"); *Field* ("August, Los Angeles, Lullaby" and "Biglietto d'Ingresso"); *The Iowa Review* ("Fairy Tale"); *Missouri Review* ("De-Icing the Wings"); *New England Review & Bread Loaf Quarterly* ("China White"); *Ploughshares* ("Anna"); *Poetry* ("The Separator" and "Sounding"); *Poetry Miscellany* ("The Way a Swan Turns"); *River Styx* ("Three Letters"). The poem "Surprise" appeared originally in *The New Yorker*.

"Fairy Tale" also appeared in *Extended Outlooks: The Iowa Review Collection of Contemporary Women Writers* (New York: Macmillan, 1981).

"Blood Hour" received the 1981 Stanley Kunitz Poetry Award from *Columbia Magazine*.

I wish to thank the John Simon Guggenheim Foundation and the National Endowment for the Arts for their support.

I would also like to thank the following individuals for their kind attention to *Wyndmere* in manuscript: Sherod Santos, Lynne McMahon, Mark Strand, Jorie Graham, Michael Ryan.

The publication of this book is supported by grants from the National Endowment for the Arts in Washington, D.C., a Federal agency, and the Pennsylvania Council on the Arts.

This book is dedicated with love and gratitude to my husband, David Dukes.

And to the memory of my grandmother, Frances Talich Kuçera.

My mother gave me my one and only birthday party when I was seven. She told me to invite everyone in the second grade class, ten children.

I remember one special thing about my party, the way my mother decorated the birthday cake. She took the purple irises from her garden and placed them on all sides of the square birthday cake. The cake had white frosting and the purple irises made a colorful frame around the cake. The irises lasted for days and gave me much joy.

Unlike peonies, which lose all their petals at once, the iris folds up gradually.

Nine years later, at my mother's funeral, the church was filled with huge bouquets of peonies and by the time the services were over, they were wilted, the petals had all fallen off, and were scattered around the vases.

—E. K. Muske

CONTENTS

I

WYNDMERE, WINDEMERE

"Weep, for the world's wrong."
—*Dirge*, Shelley

The world's wrong, mother,
Shelley said it when, at the end,
he got it right. And you, who knew
every word of his by heart, agreed.

The washed dresses stood on thin air.
You plucked them with distracted grace,
a wind-mother, a plane appearing
between the sun and me, its wings spread

in a stunned arc where the mind still
trails in bright windows of vertigo:
you held me close, you let me go.

We sat on the back step and read
together, not like two, but one
being split apart in some dream
abattoir: I could feel that violence

shudder under my nails, and looked away
from the page, as if the backyard,
the blue stalks of rhubarb, the red
swing, could stop the invisible

passage of one being through another,
the march of infant clothes
on the line, beheaded.

You said, "I'm a tough farm girl
from Wyndmere, nothing fazes me."
Nothing fazed me either, I said.
You drew your town in the dust,

3

then the thin spires of wind
that grew so tall they split
us up. Now, on a plane, I fly
beside myself. I read

because you said to. The years
pull, dazed as a line of print,
afloat in the life jacket of prose.
Poetry's the air we drown in together,

mother, poetry's the turning room,
the clear field mined with words
you read first. In Wyndmere, you said,
federal men waited by the dry well

with a paper, with justice
that could turn you outlaw.
In the wind, on the back step,
I heard the words of poets

who got it right again and again,
in a world so wrong,
it measures only loss
in those crosses of thin air,

in the blowdown and ascent
of the separator, the mother,
whose face catches once,
then turns from me, again and again.

THE SEPARATOR

My grandfather was
a Separator Man,
harvesting the wheat

in Wyndmere.
Behind his team
of stubborn plugs

rolled a machine,
an iron dinosaur
on wheels, a thresher

run by steam
that, like a man,
ate and defecated—

but had judgment
in its gut.
It separated

strong from weak
wheat from chaff—
by sunset, spread

prim fans of grain
in windrows across
the red earth.

Famous in all
the Dakota counties
where Wyndmere

had once been famous
for nothing, it
perfected itself

like some genius
of detachment,
some mechanical

moving Buddha,
it left gold temples
shuddering in its wake.

My grandfather died
rich and didn't know it.
No one told him.

By then,
he was too good
at separating—

his wife ten years dead,
his children gone away.
No one to give something to,

no one to witness how
what was taken away
stayed with him—

like the dream
of his dead wife
in his arms, asleep

in the beautiful whorls
of chaff. I remember
he held one arm

close to his side
and squinted, near-sighted,
separating the outline

of one thing
from another.
Separating

poor from poorer,
hard from stone,
the clear edible grain

from what is thrown away
to the wind
which can find

a use for anything.

YOU COULD

I didn't know you
at first, your face
in the mirror instead

of mine, that night
they put me in your room
to sleep. You stared back

still young in manner,
your smile fixed, but
defiant, sensual as

the chokecherries red
in their tart suspension
below in the root cellar

where the dusty jars
still bore your fingerprints.
You could smile like

your daughter, my mother could
and I can now, thinking how
as the mirror slowly

returned to me, you had no
white dress the night
you drove with him

to the justice. How the moon
must have rumpled the carriage
robe. How the little jewels

in my ears glittered
that night in yours.
Past the tall marquee

of silence that said
your names. Past the sheaves
of grain, past the stopped

town clock, into your dreaming
abduction of each other.
He put his hand on your shoulder

as you rode back through
the first light that placed
the silos, one by one,

in the grim fire of succession.
You watched him touch up
the horse's trot, then lift

the sun on the point of his whip.
I believe that we can annul sunrise.
I believe sometimes when the horizon

holds light too extravagantly,
like the brow of a fake jewel,
a cheap wedding band

crushed under a father's heel,
a pair of thin eager signatures
torn back into two names, I can see

the sun stopping
at the window
of the last room

he had the will
to be human in.
Within, he draws

the rope tight
over the rafter
knots it, examining

in his palm, each
monotonous shock
of the rope's braid,

split and twisted
around nothing but
the power to repeat itself.

Lying in your bed, I felt
his pure obsession set to
yours. By his own hand, he

married you forever.
So you must have brushed
your hair in the mirror

each night, my grandfather
behind you, his eyes finding
yours in the glass, where

they waited, already wed,
gone nowhere. I saw it then—
the stopped clock, the moon's

light preemptory, your lips
repeating it as if it were true:
till death.

BLOOD HOUR

The long grass blows flat
as I pass through it, dreaming,
with my taller brother and the .22.
He is teaching me how to handle a rifle.

Early sunset rakes across our path:
three burning clouds, the great
chieftains, rise above us.

When I look through the sight
I see the door opening miles away
across the plains, a woman setting
an old cradle out on her porch.

My brother puts his arm around
my shoulders from behind, his head
cocked next to mine—adjusting
the arm's cantilever, adjusting
as much as he can, the crooked line of fire

that I will see, in reverse,
from the next second forward:
from the cradle to the burning island
on which we stand—
from the dead bullet to the barrel
and back into the live shell chamber.

FAIRY TALE

In that country sacred to the wolf,
the mill no longer grinds out
its dull bread and duller proverbs.

The unshepherded flocks complain
in the empty fields. In the dead
branches sit crows too exhausted to fly.

It's November, as it has been for years.
In the kitchen of the lonely palace,
one chop hobbles into the skillet.

The barrel staves split, and stack.
High on the landing of the great staircase
above the ballroom, the chandelier

rattles its glass skeletons
and the cobweb's drawn back:
here is the illegitimate daughter of the king

standing the way she stood
the night he banished her,
cold-eyed, her gray cloak slipping

from her shoulder—as she strikes
her open palm with the riding crop—
to emphasize each point she is making.

According to the story, it's her job,
now that she's back, to make the leaves
regrow, to unfreeze the waterfall.

Why does she wait?
All she has to do is speak the ancient name
of each predator
                    and he will open his eyes,
walk on his hind legs through the gate,
looking right and left, clean-shaven,

utterly certain of a second chance.

CHINA WHITE

—M. S. H.

Lately your eyes watch me
out of animal eyes,
out of the sad clerk's eyes
at the makeup counter.
She didn't have the right shade
of shadow, but I charged to my account
the kind of green I chide myself with.

I kept thinking—
Why did you take so long to cry?
You were just fifteen
when it happened.
Still, you insisted on indifference,
like the Stoics, you said.

Next day, in class, leaves fell
from your Latin book.
He had gloves on, you said later,
when I held you, in that strange room
where you finally wept.
There were leaves beneath,
I couldn't breathe.

As usual, I got you laughing—
we made up our eyes,
you disembodied your gaze
with China White, and gray.

You didn't cry again.
That night you sang the Magnificat
for Glee. It wasn't in your voice
to rephrase the Virgin's words
but there's a part where she accepts it,
accepts the miracle they want her body for

and your eyes came looking for mine
as you sang, moving slowly at first,
then faster: face to face to face.

THE WAY A SWAN TURNS

in purposeful white speed,
the way the Best Man, drunk,
doffs his hat to the swan . . .

Like lovers in a duel of intuition,
they drift and burn, standing apart.
As if he'd never knelt in the darkness,

calling, as if she'd never risen,
shattering the clear surface
to eat slowly from his hand.

The wind sculpts itself into distance,
the drunk bows, the swan glides away
under the trees bent with age,

beneath the lifted swords of the statues.
I turn away from the window in my white dress
to the hinged mirror where

I become a procession of brides.
My mother stands, fastening
her long light hair with pins—

her hand moving so fast, it exceeds
gesture, a limb burning, its fingers
opening into a fan of flame.

You don't let people love you she says.
Let the mirror scatter its affections,
let me lift my glass, let him stand by my side,

with the others, one by one, let them love me
as I loved the sun igniting the veil
as we walk in the park after the ceremony.

Enigmatic as a bride, she turns to me,
twisting the ring on her finger, veiling
her face in the purest lack of emphasis,

in the face of love's fiercest commandment:
let them touch you
Look how the swan turns and turns on the blue pond.

The sky fills with invisible comets.
The carousel flings itself round a painted center
from which the wooden horses shy,

lifting their hooves, their torn eyes,
to the mechanized ceiling
where the gears raise

and lower them like skulls
on pikes, like her face
turning away from mine

in rapt sequence: mirror,
snowfall, swan, mother,
one little love after another.

A FORMER LOVE, A LOVER OF FORM

When they kiss,
she feels a certain revulsion,
and as they continue to kiss

she enters her own memory
carrying a wicker basket
of laundry. As the wind lifts,

the clothes wrap themselves
around her: damp sleeves
around her neck, stockings

in her hair. Gone her schoolgirl's
uniform, the pale braids and body
that went anywhere anonymously.

Her glasses fall forward on her nose,
her mouth opens: all around
are objects that desire, suddenly, her.

Not just clothes, but open doorways,
love seats, Mother's bright red
espadrilles kicked off in the damp grass.

If she puts on lipstick, she'll lie
forever. But she's too nearsighted,
you see, she doesn't spot the wind

approaching in a peach leisure suit—
or the sheer black nightie swaying
from a branch. Is she seducer or seduced?

And which is worse,
a dull lover's kiss or the embrace
of his terrible laundry?

She'd rather have the book
he wrote than him.

SURPRISE

The mind dislikes surprise.
Witness the nurse of good syntax,
how she pushes her drugged charges
across the courtyard below
to the Center for Impaired Speech.

Witness the doorman hesitating
before ringing your bell to tell you
someone's on the way up.

It's why you're getting up slowly
this morning, why you don't look too closely
at the mirror, nor the coffee table
offering its testimony: the matches

crippled in their books, crushed by
the insistent pressure of thumb and forefinger,
the empty fifth, the Zig Zag litter,
the pages of unclothed women, legs apart,

smiling out as if there were no danger
in this world, even from those you love.
And from those who love you in ways you have
not yet imagined—and which might surprise you,

like a style of perverse instruction
say, teaching the blind pornography,
their trained fingers hesitating above
the machined welts of braille.

It is possible to teach someone that love
is pain—by taking a fistful of hair, pulling
it up from the skull and back, till the neck
locks in place, as if breaking, till the lover

stops thinking about politics, or the five days
of fine weather—and begins to cooperate
with this gesture, applied one night
in passion, the next in pure rage.

Still, the mind is stubborn, resists
the unexpected—shuttling back and forth,
as it was taught, between similar forms—refusing
in the only way it knows how, to make sense.

So you sit this morning, while the mail comes,
and the *Times*, the phone rings and you can touch
your hair, your face, rethinking it all—

        but recall your horror once
opening the front door, on your birthday, on seeing the faces
of your friends disfigured by the weight of occasion.
You thought the ones who liked you least screamed loudest:
Surprise!

ILLNESS AS METAPHOR

Severn described them, after your death,
"brutal Italians," burning the furniture,
scraping the walls of the little room

off the Piazza di Spagna. They'd scrub
TB away, as if disease were a badly
expressed idea: erased and forgotten.

One hundred fifty years later they
offer for sale a page in your hand.

Sign here, John Keats, you'll like
your new apartment: great view
of the Spanish Steps, best dope

in Rome. And a bladelike somnolence
after noon, like a clock's hand falling
in shadow over the dozers on the steps—

a little Vatican of sighs rising, where,
upstairs, fans gather over a lock of your hair.

Here, this fine morning, late August,
the air a telephoto lens drawing toward us
those walking away—I can magnify many times

these bodies in their silk prints and sun-
glasses, but their souls drift in permanent
transience, in the light-distance of God's photograph,

which some call Poetry, when they adjust
the eye to an optical illusion which allows
us to see. You saw. Soul and illusion.

Ah, the twentieth century, ah the nineteenth.
One heartless, the other literal-
minded about love. You guessed which

was which as you lay above, coughing
your lungs into a cup, looking out
at the grand escalier, the sky extending

its blue canopy, thinking,
it's a picture, this world.
Let me go on a little longer.

Signori, finding your face
on the good wall of the page.

Here are the keys, John Keats,
the rent's due on the first,
and the last, as you drift—

alive and dying—gone forever
and just now climbing up the great
stairs, troubled and pale, your

long hair blowing, crying,
Signori, how much for this room?

UNHEARD OF

We sat talking those long afternoons
in a kitchen, under a ceiling of greenery.
Because you happened to be in the body of a man,
and I, in a woman's, we made love sometimes,

because it was a way
to say something right,
something written in us
that could only be read
by the light of the other.

Once you put your hands on my head
to heal its aching, for no reason
other than *mothering*, a gift unheard of in a man.

This was many years ago,
before I understood how
we long, in our passions,
to be observed failing, then saved.
An act of medicine.

The wind blew around that old house,
remember? and snow fell,
but I felt better and better.

It was tropical sometimes,
the lazy rhododendron unfurling
one green leaf, then another.

There rose the gold steam of tea,
there were your fingertips on my temples—
unlike morphine, holding its blue-veined gloves
above the long scarred keyboard—

you exacted it, the pain
that would fail precisely into memory:
the moving leaves, the sun shining
on the text of human suffering,

the difference between disease and symptom,
or symptom and cure, *for rubella,*
for cholera, for petit mal,
for fôlie à deux
                and scrawled on the flyleaf,
your name in bold relief,
Healton, Edward B.

ANNA

Too hot to sleep,
she watches the night
clouds haul their stalled
evaporate overhead,

and below, on the lawn,
sprinklers rain
around themselves.
She's twelve,

she's just read *Karenina*,
and now the world's
a margin, the edge

of a better text.
                Below,
in the dusk, a woman
about to give birth

waits on the porch,
waits outside what
she feels, aware of
the body's comic aristocracy:

the shocked profile
above the belly, the belly
above the poor frightened feet.
She glances upstairs,

but upstairs there is
only Anna, who has given
her arm to the Commissar
of Darkness, her sleeve

brushing the sleeve
of the page with fire.
         The living page
crossed with blood

just one week before
by Raskolnikov—
                  the print
ground like a servant's

studded heel in the face
of the status quo. So
what if this far south
of Siberia, the Aurora

diminishes to the cramped neon
                  of a bar,
or here in the suburbs,
one star?

         The neighbors' houses
loom dark as the inside of
a suitcase. The siren peels
its poisonous fruit, the seeds

scattering from the grave of Emma B.,
a black rain duplicating each pore
in her beautiful whore's face,
the absolute pronoun of that oval.

It will come to all of us,
the sky's empty parking lot
filled with glittering cinders,
the stillborn, the dead one,

standing next to each of us,
then aside. Like her eye
on the page, moving down the hall
on the arm of the blood machine,

the black dress walking on its own
to the hammered rails,
                    these words
waving two ways on the page,

like prayer,
           thank God
who with this book
in my hands

             keeps talking to me.

AFTERWARDS

After our short flight together,
we boarded separate planes
and flew to opposite ends of the country.

The first flight was rough,
you held me and later,
alone on the longer one, I recalled

the perfect gravity of your embrace,
and fell asleep, my dream blooming
backwards into the gentle silks of a chute.

Now, afterwards, I feel like I'm moving
obedient to some physical law people
believe in, but can never describe,
like the principle of air flowing over
the wings of a plane, allowing it to rise.

You sat beside me, holding me to
a perfect understatement of myself,
the way sign language understates thought
rediscovering it in the body.

Here, in another country, your thought
still holds me. You turn,
you say my name to me—
while the plane banks, as the tower dictates.

It has something to do with the power of loss,
how it opposes itself at the last moment.
It has to do with how the plane, lifting off
from this world reluctantly, reappears above it,
effortless in flight. It has to do with how

your lips felt smiling against my ear,
how you held me as we fell,
how falling together, our lives
seemed the only constant objects in the sky

and how impossible it seemed
that thin air would ever
begin to displace us.

DE-ICING THE WINGS

They are de-icing the Eastern shuttle.
Men in yellow masks stand on the wings
in the hard sleet and hose gold smoke
over the hold. The book on Cubism
in her hands shakes when they rev the jets.

She is going somewhere to teach somebody something,
to talk to people sitting in solemn rows,
an orchard of note-takers, writing the words
dadaist disassociation over and over.

She can't find the page in her lecture notes
where Bergson says an image is the visual equivalent
of a musical chord . . . so maybe she can just walk
into the classroom, throw away the book and say:

Here's what your teacher did wrong in her life—
and here's what's wrong out there on the runway.

Look how we try to de-ice the surface,
in large-handed, smoky swipes at intimacy,
not getting down to the fragile metal,
the trouble-armor which, under nonstop,
high stress, disintegrates in thin air!

Something like these hands, students,
which have not held another body with love
in weeks. They hold the book to the heart,
defensively. They keep the fine, stylized
stream of interrogation flowing close
to the text, providing a pure reading of intention

similar to the recognition of hunger in another.
Or like a description of passion in language
utterly riveting, where what the author desires
beats so near to the surface.

If you love literature, question its critics—
who are to that beautiful effort as landing
gear and flaps are to the wings—

still extended beneath your teacher, holding up
as always, growing warmer now, by degrees.

BIGLIETTO D'INGRESSO

I rented a house
in the old Roman wall
in Barbarino Val d'Elsa.
It was like a treehouse

overlooking the wine blue valley
and faraway, the towers of San Gimignano.
Three stories down, beneath the stones
of the street, slept a few
of the town's Etruscans, city fathers,
happily buried below year
after year of the famous chianti.

The day I arrived
I sat in a red chair
and looked out the windows
at the olive trees
and thought of August.

How the house, like a month
in a year, kept its privacy,
its calendar address,
guarded its doors, front
and back, as if each day

made a family of watchers,
then a family of revelers,
as the presses in the winery
made liquor from the hobbled vines.

Out of that crude useful mouth
as from the hand of the Lord
came the bounty of harvest,

the single light by which
the books of reckoning are read.

Already there was a familiar
still life I'd composed around
my solitude, laying my knife
across the plate like a hunter
discarding his weapon in the sun
next to a stream, watching it
become the brightest object

in the landscape. I watched
the scirocco leave the trees
trembling, one by one,
brushing them with studied casualness,
like people stroking the hair of orphans—

as if loss, in its beauty,
was an accusation, growing
stronger with each act of careless attention.

I stalked what the wind said,
tree by tree, I stalked grief—
but grief didn't want me—

like the homeless child in the street,
her face a little mirror held up
against each solicitous expression:

Grief didn't need me, it never did.
Grief had other subjects,
Grief had doors carved in the great churches.
Grief had its family.

So what was I thinking of
that morning I left the Uffizi early,
the ticket of admission forgotten
in my hand? I was going

to meet you. It wasn't yet noon,
but we were already in the day
kept private by every night
we did not know each other.

As I walked, I saw
the kitchen of my crooked house
in the trees. On the sideboard,
a pair of scales that tipped,

off balance, letting a handful
of fava beans outweigh a loaded coin,
a lead counterweight, and hang,
trembling like each space

the wind vacates. When we shook
hands, the stamped ticket fluttered
away and I was happy to see

all around us, paintings
of the local miracles: the saints
who cheated no one, but believed
in making things even, occasionally,
in this world of inequity.

The light was perfect that day.
I can see us clearly, weighing
each other below the mild eyes
of the saint, the orphans and the ill,
transformed by Giotto into angels.

All along the street and at
the doors of the embassy
were those same children who
belong to no one, not even grief

and I see now
how the angel of justice
spins in the painter's eye
tips the ancient scale

in favor of the left hand, the fistful
of fava, the lopsided smile, the dirty
curls, the stunted lamb, the crooked door
of love, opening where we stand
that second before recovering,
at our feet, held still in the wind,
the *biglietto d'ingresso.*

A FRESCO

All day I've been thinking of the grief
on each of their faces, Adam and Eve.

The feeling is closest to a wave as it peaks,
how it seems on the verge of self-consciousness

before it collapses. Their mouths hold
a single sound that divides, familiar as rain.

The angel points away from the green world
behind them, out into the nave. I remember

the woman standing there, turned to stone
at the side altar, and the man next to her,

the back of his overcoat on fire with
reflected light. They stared straight ahead

at The Expulsion and the cruel, distinct words
passed between them. Tourists, a corsage at her heart,

his brand new guidebook. What is startling
is how the fresco works itself out from under

the expectation of color. After a while
in this air the other spectrum emerges:

no blues or reds but grades of dark and eerie
white, as the paint thins and the lead extracts

new expressions. They never raised their voices.
The woman seemed like someone who had been loved,

but without compassion. I don't know about the man.
I recall the rest of that church now, how

with small fierce gestures, votive fires
were lit. The two figures burning in effigy.

III

THREE LETTERS

I. From the Arsonist

The women in prison merge,
arrange themselves in rows.
No one will yield easily
to the other—except

the arsonist, the woman
who is afraid to speak
and who is beaten. She
yields to everybody.
She follows each shape
their bodies succeed,

her eyes a sentry torch,
a spark pinched into service.
Light is wrenched from her face,
like some brutal ornament of the familiar.

God has told her every sin
and she will remember each one
in her further radiance.

God folds back the metal gates,
the guard pokes the burning eye
of a lighter to her smoke.

There is a gold chain of vertebrae
she can count through the thin skin
of the cloth in front of her.

If she thinks at all,
she thinks of the singed wall
of breath, the heart's inferno.
Hell is the absence of metaphor.

II. To J.

When we sat side by side at the play,
I could feel you clearing the way
through the skeptic's monologue to faith.

Two nuns and the voice of reason.
Reason, as always, a second-rate performance—
but I could sense you beside me ordering
those two opposing styles of imagination:

till innocence in its cloud
restored evil, as it does,
restored the wordy god
who impersonates us.

Once I sat around a table with four
lady murderers, on Riker's Island
each Friday night, we wrote poetry.

Crime was a way of composing the spirit.
Sally Chester described God's voice
making her walk three times round

her drunk husband as he slumped
head down on the kitchen table.
She kissed both temples before

blowing his head off. So what
if he'd beaten her ten years
running, the jury saw her

unraveling like a used fabric,
three times around that table,

  like the woman
who lifted her baby out
of the window high up

in the projects, the thread
between them didn't snap because
she could fly —

       Crime
is never crime as it happens,
it's ritual, the uglier for
not recognizing itself:

the gauzy shoulders ripped
from the real shoulders, once,
twice, the facsimile of a lover's
face painted in blood
on a mirror.

Here, the poor hands of the actress
are drenched
in God's cosmetic.

The playwright
has her kill her baby
quick—it is his
signature,
the swift dénouement:

the exact reverse of a miracle,
though a miracle was hoped for
having been held in abeyance
awaiting God's pure instructions.

III. To Lee, in L.A.

Back in New York,
I put bread on the fire escape
for the small gang of birds
who congregate there.

45

It is the simplest offering
I know to the god of hunger,

        and joy.
The sun, which has lost everything,
and so long ago, shines on us.
The wind lifts its hands
over its small fliers
as they land and eat.
One by one. I divide myself

now between love and fear,
like David, learning his lines,
staring at me out of the mind
of a long-dead composer.
The day after Curtis and I

each bought an electric rose
at Radio City, I put mine
in the vase with the real flowers
near the window where the birds scatter.

where the soul, that chimney sweep,
can blow aside the ashes and find
the last small fire that we are.
To imagine a child, sparrow,
a small fire. To be granted

that blessing and the further
blessing to accept it, Lord,
this great mercy I ask of you.

WHITE KEY

The mountains shut their doors
in the shadow of the jet
turning east over the continent—

widening like the light on the bed
in the blue room where I last held
someone I loved. Out there

the palms line up, straight
and bent as rain, but the leaves
and the red bird's question

at each descending step of sleep
bring on my prison dream—
where escape is an ongoing joke,

where the inmate tunnels furiously
and thinks he's free, while above
ground, the tower lights track

his burrowing. See the good trees
lean down, lowering their nooses?
I could tell you I don't dream

that dream anymore. That when
I walked through the warning
on the door, I woke. Still, the sun

inched a barred shadow
forward to the glass doors
I slid open this morning,

and with human lives inside,
the plane now circles above
Manhattan. At downward distance,

under roof after roof,
the mind lies to itself
and tries to sleep, the body

bends into its conscious cage.
The plane hovers over its
perfectly marked lines

of entry, as thought flies
parallel to revelation,
dreaming of all the places

along its body it might
intersect with sudden light.
But doesn't. The man sleeping

next to me holds his whiskey
to his heart. Say the plane
is a white key turning in

the sky's white ignition.
Say what fires the air
is not the tarred surface

below, runged with spun treads,
but release from the descending world,
the only one we know, and the false

gold god of the horizon
we worshipped all night,
all wrong. I turn to you

in my mind. Behind us,
door after door turns
to solid wall in space.

WE DRIVE THROUGH TYNDALL'S
THEORY OF SIGHT

—David

That day we drove for hours—
the blue clouds sculpted against the point
hundreds of miles away where architecture
seemed a promise. Still, as far as I can see,
we live in landscapes half-remembered:

the milky haze, the upturned eyes
of other lovers, light refracting
the impurities that make us
visible to each other. The air itself
a form of resistance, a white grid

of retrospect—where a snowfall
of shadows shifts, forms people
we once knew, so perfect in their flaws.
Here is the world's skeleton: the ossified
white we have to imagine inside the body

clouded by such green eyes, such red lips,
a T-shirt that says DREAM ON. They could
make a movie of it: people who were mistakes,
people who held sentiment in fear, hostages
of their own commonness. Here, the horizon

seems to reenter itself and sing,
the way it once seemed to Sappho
at dusk addressing the Pleiades.
She looked at that rising city
and saw two things: stars made of dust

and those divine sisters made of the same.
This is the way the poet saw and I say
you're perfect because I love you,
and also the reverse—though I catch you
beside me, shifting into fifth, with a beauty

49

Poe called supernal, feelings attached.
Make something of it, I dare you who read this.
We go forward into pure light, which
I am familiar with, though I also know
the Fat Man and the fox-faced woman,

I'm familiar with it all. This is as close
as we get on this earth, going forward,
transformed, into distance remembered.

Tyndall's Effect: that impurities in the air allow us to see light.

COMING OVER COLDWATER

I drive fast, uphill
& static picks what the radio plays
to pieces. The palms are idle, spotlit,
above the occasional court a late wind pays

their crowns. On shifting lots
to the canyon top, houses built on chance
zigzag like lines of coke on a mirror.
One too close to the other and no insurance

for big sliders. Still, something
permanent waits here to reclaim itself:
solar panels hoard the sun, under a redwood,
a woman at her kiln stares at the fiery shelf.

It's no safe harbor. What is?
When it blows, the Santa Ana blows
right down to the brick, but like
the green spike of mint or marjoram

faded into a stew, there's a hint
of original taste here. The scent
of what these slowly falling neighbors
cook in one pot, but apart, meditates

in the air, sort of Moroccan.
In the dead eye of the brights, I spot
red tiles, a way of life. I like it.
Offstage, Mother Pacific turns up

her thousand winged collars.
Further out, is a Zen ring
of islands, air-brushed, fanned up
like sand from a wind machine, where wing

51

over wing, the land lets go. I
wouldn't call it exile at all. Are you
coming home to Christ? the sign asks,
and I think of the thirty-two

years it took him to work up
an appetite for human company.
When he cried *Sitio,* I thirst,
someone offered him hyssop

on the cross. His tongue
a black dart, he turned and spoke
kindly to the person next to him.
He was happy then, promising heaven

to a thief, drinking in the earth
himself, still, its streams
and green canyon pools. *I thirst.*
Out on Coldwater, I hit low beams.

DAVID

He played a paralyzed man once,
before I knew him. He made
his body settle into
a position of broken readiness,

hunched on the rotting pins of his bones.
I thought I'd seen it before: actors
in wheelchairs as actors in wheelchairs.
But he gave that damage power,

a sound in the throat that rattled
the cast around him. Too real, I suppose,
for film, with its images fast as litter
in a ditch—but for me,

who'd been waking night after night
in a sweat of disbelief, my whole life
a Platonist double-take, sparkless
as the severed nerves of the spine,

it made sense. *Too real, I suppose,*
my moving hands on the bedclothes,
the good blood in my extremities,
some unwanted lover's love, gathered up

as he slept, into the repeating mechanism.
But that first morning, when we'd found
our way to each other, he'd already survived
my imagination and before dawn, I made

my pact with illusion. He was out
on the balcony and I thought
I heard singing. When I went out

there he stood looking over Assisi,
not a single sound but the new sun,
a day, blue and windless,
coffee and a little bread on a tray.

PANIS ANGELICUS

Here, I say, here's a little step
we call the bop, two up and two back

and Rosalina gets it right the first time.
Then there's the hustle, if you like traffic.
I like the flute heard every morning in
the courtyard. I like the tinny transmission

from Puccini's formal soul to the portable
Aldo carries. I like the two signorinas who sing
for nothing each night, arm in arm, crossing the piazza.
The heart shunts out its lifetime supply

along lines as precise and irrelevant as the old
map of a town nearby, bombed in the war, rebuilt
in modern style, not a sign of the old streets.
Not a sign of the portals, the blessed mask above.

Heaven, in the frescoes, has such an air
of distraction, all those souls intent
on their vanishing difference. Even in
the afterworld's imperial gaze, a woman

retraces the shape of her child's head,
over and over, with her imagined hands.
Maybe the body makes the soul regret
its perfectibility:

                    See how the old nun,
like a half-blind angel, follows the stream
of children from the village church? She is
guarding each pair of closed eyes, each mouth

closed over a bridling tongue on which
a sphere of flat dough, the host,
uneasily rests.

Then there is the other morning.
Bells. Rosalina on a skateboard. The skate's lame,
but it carries her so far, she says. Nearly
to the old fortification, far as the eye can follow.

AUGUST, LOS ANGELES, LULLABY

The pure amnesia of her face,
newborn. I looked so far
into her that, for a while,

the visual held no memory.
Little by little, I returned
to myself, waking to nurse

those first nights in that
familiar room where all
the objects had been altered

imperceptibly: the gardenia
blooming in the dark
in the scarred water glass,

near the phone my handwriting
illegible, the patterned lamp-
shade angled downward and away

from the long mirror where
I stood and looked at
the woman holding her child.

Her face kept dissolving
into expressions resembling
my own, but the child's was pure

figurative, resembling no one.
We floated together in the space
a lullaby makes, head to head,

half-sleeping. *Save it,*
my mother would say, meaning
just the opposite. She didn't

56

want to hear my evidence
against her terrible optimism
for me. And though, despite her,

I can redeem, in a pawnshop
sense, almost any bad moment
from my childhood, I see now

what she must have intended
for me. I felt it for *her*,
watching her as she slept,

watching her suck as she
dreamed of sucking, lightheaded
with thirst as my blood flowed

suddenly into tissue that
changed it to milk. No matter
how close I press, there is a

texture that moves between me
and whatever might have injured
us then. Like the curtain's sheer

opacity, it remains drawn
over what view we have of dawn
here in this onetime desert,

now green and replenished,
its perfect climate
unthreatened in memory—

though outside, as usual,
the wind blew, the bough bent,
under the eaves, the hummingbird

touched once the bloodcolored hourglass,
the feeder, then was gone.

SOUNDING

—Annie Cameron

Four months in the womb
you were photographed
with sound. We stared

at the pulsing surface
of your skull, your fingers
lifting, as if to stave off

a sudden wind in that
sealed room where for
so long only our two

hearts echoed each other.
Screened, your heart glowed
at the joint of the caliper.

Months later, after
they had bathed you
and brought you to me,

I washed you again—
in privacy, opened
one by one the clenched

fingers seen too soon,
brushed the thin skin
of the skull where

the brain's leaping blood
bulged against it.
For months, I'd heard it

in dreams: the underwater gong
then the regular shock waves—
an assault as barbaric as conception,

the soul rung forward into image,
as metal is stunned into coin,
as the hammer sounds against its resistance:

the gold unblinking eye of the forge.

PITT POETRY SERIES

Ed Ochester, General Editor

Shirley Kaufman, *Gold Country*
Ted Kooser, *One World at a Time*
Ted Kooser, *Sure Signs: New and Selected Poems*
Larry Levis, *Winter Stars*
Larry Levis, *Wrecking Crew*
Robert Louthan, *Living in Code*
Tom Lowenstein, tr., *Eskimo Poems from Canada and Greenland*
Archibald MacLeish, *The Great American Fourth of July Parade*
Peter Meinke, *Trying to Surprise God*
Judith Minty, *In the Presence of Mothers*
Carol Muske, *Camouflage*
Carol Muske, *Wyndmere*
Leonard Nathan, *Dear Blood*
Leonard Nathan, *Holding Patterns*
Kathleen Norris, *The Middle of the World*
Sharon Olds, *Satan Says*
Greg Pape, *Black Branches*
Greg Pape, *Border Crossings*
Thomas Rabbitt, *Exile*
James Reiss, *Express*
Ed Roberson, *Etai-Eken*
Eugene Ruggles, *The Lifeguard in the Snow*
Dennis Scott, *Uncle Time*
Herbert Scott, *Groceries*
Richard Shelton, *Of All the Dirty Words*
Richard Shelton, *Selected Poems, 1969-1981*
Richard Shelton, *You Can't Have Everything*
Gary Soto, *Black Hair*
Gary Soto, *The Elements of San Joaquin*
Gary Soto, *The Tale of Sunlight*
Gary Soto, *Where Sparrows Work Hard*
Tomas Tranströmer, *Windows & Stones: Selected Poems*
Chase Twichell, *Northern Spy*
Constance Urdang, *The Lone Woman and Others*
Constance Urdang, *Only the World*
Ronald Wallace, *Tunes for Bears to Dance To*
Cary Waterman, *The Salamander Migration and Other Poems*
Bruce Weigl, *A Romance*
David P. Young, *The Names of a Hare in English*
Paul Zimmer, *Family Reunion: Selected and New Poems*